Asking for Trouble 3

SHERRYL CLARK

Illustrated by Kristin Headlam

Triple3Play

Published by
Sundance Publishing
One Beeman Road
P.O. Box 740
Northborough, MA 01532-0740

First published 1999 as Supa Dazzlers by
Addison Wesley Longman Australia Pty Limited
95 Coventry Street
South Melbourne 3205 Australia
Exclusive United States Distribution: Sundance Publishing

ISBN 0-7608-4803-3

Contents

Chapter 1

I couldn't believe it. Almost summer, and we'd been here close to a year. Sometimes it felt like six years. I still wasn't a country kid.

"What are you writing now?" I asked.

My younger sister Julie chewed the top of her pink pen. "A letter to Natalie."

"Not another one." Natalie had just been down for the weekend. When Mom drove her back to the city, I wasn't allowed to go.

"You've got homework to finish," Mom said. But I knew she thought once I got to the city, I'd want to stay with my friends. She was right.

I heard a high-pitched whistle out in the street. It was Kenny on his bike.

"You coming?" he called.

"Where to?"

"Down to the river for a swim."

I grabbed an old towel and climbed on my bike. Just below the bridge there was a large pool at the bend of the river. Someone had strung a rope there from a big willow tree. It was so cool, swinging way out above the water and letting go. It was almost like flying.

After we'd done that about twenty times each, Kenny and I sat back on the riverbank in the short grass.

"Are you going on the city-camp field trip this year?" Kenny asked.

"What's that?"

"Middle school kids usually go to the city for three days. Except this year there's not enough money, so we're just going for one day. It'll probably be boring, but anything's better than school."

"Yeah. What do you do? Go shopping?"

"No, we're going to some science museum." Kenny poked me. "But you wouldn't want to go to the city, would you?"

"I sure would." I stared up at the clouds, imagining one was a big white bus, taking me back to where I belonged—where all my friends were. Even if none of them had written to me, I couldn't wait. "When are we going?"

"In a couple of weeks. Didn't your mom get the field-trip form from school?"

"No. Well, she didn't say anything."

"Maybe she won't let you go," said Kenny.

"Why not? I've been good for ages," I said. It helped having Kenny as a friend. The other kids weren't too bad, except big-mouth Ben, and he mostly kept away from me now. I got the feeling Kenny had warned him off.

"Your mom's a bit of a mind reader," Kenny grinned at me. "She probably thinks you're going to run off again."

"No way. It wouldn't be worth the risk. Ms. Crawson would give me detention for six months."

But already I was planning the whole thing.

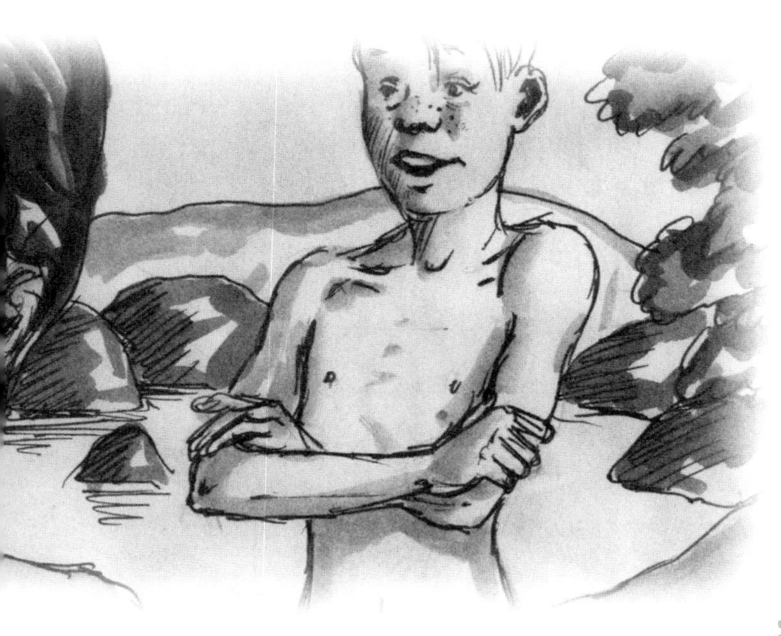

Chapter 2

At school on Monday, I got another copy of the field-trip form and took it home, pretending this was the first I'd heard of it.

"Mom, can you sign this field-trip form for me, please?"

She read it and frowned. "I'm not sure this is a good idea."

"Why not? That science museum sounds great. Ms. Crawson told us all about it." She

hadn't yet, but I knew she would. Ms. Crawson was a great believer in preparation.

Mom stared at me suspiciously. "Can I trust you to stay out of trouble and not run off?"

I avoided answering that. "We're going on the bus and having lunch in the cafeteria. I just have to take a drink."

"Hmmmm." She took forever to make up her mind, but finally she said, "All right, you can go. But if you cause any trouble, look out!"

"Yes, Mom."

I kept a straight face all through dinner, then raced off to my room. In my top drawer, I found some quarters and added them to the fifty cents that Mom had given me for an afternoon snack. I snuck out the back door and ran down to the public telephone near the gas station.

The phone rang for ages, and I was beginning to think maybe Tron wasn't home. At last someone answered.

"Hello?" I said. "Is Tron there?"

"Just a minute." Tron finally picked up the phone. "Hello?" He sounded a long way away.

"It's me—Leo."

"Er . . . Leo? Marrelli?"

"Yeah, Leo Marrelli! Who else? Listen, I'm coming back. Can you meet me?"

"You're moving back here? How come?"

"Well, not moving exactly. I'll explain when I see you. How about we meet at the mall? Tell all the others to come, too." I told him the date and time, but he sounded funny. "Can you make it, Tron?"

"Maybe. I don't know. Dad's been on my case about skipping school. But I'll tell Nick and Tony, OK?"

It wasn't OK. I thought he'd be really excited to hear from me and want to hang out together again. I hung up, feeling kind of disappointed, and walked home.

Chapter 3

Baseball Mania

What if none of them turned up? No, of course they'd come. They were my friends. Wait until I told them about big-mouth Ben and how I'd flattened him. Well, sort of.

I cheered myself up thinking of all the stories I could tell them—about the tiny school, and fishing and swimming, and how small this whole place was.

At school the next day, Ms. Crawson started training our baseball team for the inter-school competition. We all had to try out for positions.

"Leo, you can try out first for pitcher," she said. Behind her back, Ben glared at me and walked off to third base, where Ms. Crawson had assigned him. "Kenny, first base. Bos, you can try catcher."

I pitched the ball hard and fast, but I couldn't get it over the plate, no matter how I tried.

"Ben, your turn." He smirked and walked over to me, his hand out for the ball.

"Let an expert show you how, Slicker," he said.

I dropped the ball on the ground. "Oops, it slipped," I said.

Ms. Crawson put me in as catcher. Great, I thought. Ben will probably try to take my head off. But he didn't. He was dead serious about his pitching, no fooling around—and he was really good. So I found myself concentrating and catching like a pro. At the end of practice, Ms. Crawson announced the team.

Kenny was first baseman, Ben was pitcher, I was catcher. Ringo and Sally had hit four home runs each during tryouts, so we had an ace team.

We played baseball nonstop for the next two weeks. Kenny and Ben and I agreed to practice together after school every day, too. I wasn't too sure about that, but Ben actually started acting OK. Being a good pitcher had turned him into a different person. I couldn't quite figure it out, but I was relieved he wasn't giving me a hard time anymore.

We were so wrapped up in baseball, I forgot about the school field trip. Suddenly, it was the day before we were due to go. In class Ms. Crawson said, "Now remember, you'll need a notebook and pen, a drink, and a jacket, just in case." She glared at us all, one by one, and everyone squirmed in their seats. "There will be *no* fighting on the bus, and *everyone* will stay with his or her group at the science museum. *Am I making myself clear?"*

We all nodded. I thought about my plan to sneak off, and shivered. What would Ms. Crawson do to me? Too bad, I was going. I'd waited too long to see Tron and Tony and Nick. No one was stopping me now.

"Stay out of trouble, Leo," Mom said the next morning. "I'm trusting you."

That made me feel guilty for a few minutes, but it soon wore off. "Yes, Mom." I threw my gear in my backpack and added some photos Mom had taken of Kenny and me down at the river. I was ready.

Chapter 4

The Great Escape

The first part of the bus trip took forever. Then I started to see familiar landmarks—planes taking off from the airport, the car factory, the skyscrapers. The science museum was only a short train ride away from the mall where I'd arranged to meet Tron. I had money in my pocket for the fare.

The bus driver parked near the main entrance, and we climbed out and lined up. Ms. Crawson paid for our tickets, our hands were stamped, and we walked into the first section, where there were cars and airplanes everywhere.

"Hey, this is cool," said Kenny. "I've always wanted to see what the engines in these old cars looked like."

"Yeah," I agreed, glancing around to check out the best escape route.

Kenny poked me. "What are you up to?"

"Nothing. Just looking," I protested.

"Yeah, sure," he said. "You're taking off, aren't you?"

"Ssshh," I hissed. "Tell the whole world, why don't you?"

"I'm coming with you."

"No, you're not."

"Yes, I am."

"You're not."

Just then, Ms. Crawson loomed over us. "What are you boys waiting for? Get your notebooks out and start in this section. Don't forget that you'll have to write a report on the part you liked best."

She gathered another group in a bunch and started explaining to them why it rains. I turned and slipped behind one of the cars, then headed for the exit.

Outside, I started walking fast, pretending I was any normal kid going to get something he'd forgotten on the bus. My heart was thumping like a hamster trying to get out of its cage. I passed the bus and turned the first corner. Then I felt a hand on my shoulder.

"You can slow down now." It was Kenny.

"I told you not to come," I snapped. "I'll get blamed for getting you in trouble, too."

He shrugged. "Nah. I'm bigger than you. I'll say it was my idea."

"Like my mom will believe that!"

"Who cares? Might as well have a good time. Where are we going?"

I explained. "I'm supposed to meet them at twelve."

"Let's go then," he said.

I had to admit I didn't really mind Kenny tagging along. I pointed out all the familiar things—things I hadn't seen for ages. He liked the train's doors, and when we got to the mall he murmured, "My mom would go crazy in here. She loves clothes stores."

I was busy looking for Tron. We'd agreed to meet near the fountain, but I couldn't see him anywhere. Surely he hadn't forgotten? I should have called him again.

"What's that?" Kenny pointed at a shish kebab rotating over a grill.

"They're great. Do you like garlic?"

He screwed up his nose. "No. Maybe I'll just get a hamburger. I'm starving." He wandered off to buy one, and I waited by the fountain,

SOUVLAK
HAMBUR

feeling like I was getting pins and needles in my legs. Where was Tron?

"Hey, Leo!" It was Nick.

"Hi, Nick. Where are Tron and Tony?"

"They couldn't come—they said to say sorry. Tron's in trouble for skipping school, and Tony's away at his aunt's."

"Oh." It had all been for nothing then. I stared at the floor, my shoulders hunched.

Chapter 5

Trouble

"I'm here, though," Nick laughed, and it sounded funny—a bit fake. "I'm not worried about school. Haven't been for a week."

"Oh." I looked at him more closely. He seemed different; his clothes were scruffy, and his hair hung around his face.

"Who's your friend?"

Kenny had returned with his hamburger. "This is Kenny. He lives near me. We go to the same school. We ditched the field trip together. Kenny, this is Nick."

"Hi." Kenny suddenly got very interested in his hamburger.

"Let's go, then," Nick said. "I've got to pick up something for my mom. You might as well come, too. Show Kenny the arcade and some sights."

"Oh, OK." I was saying "oh" an awful lot. I sounded like a real idiot.

We followed Nick out the back entrance of the mall and up a side street. Kenny finished eating and gazed around. "Where's the arcade you told me about?"

"Over that way." Nick waved his hand. "We'll go there later." Kenny didn't talk after that, so I filled the silence by jabbering on about where I used to ride my bike and how to get to my old house.

When Nick stopped suddenly, we nearly walked into him. "This is where my mom's friend lives," he said. "I've got to pick up something around back. You wait here, OK?"

"Sure," I nodded.

"I won't be long." Just as he was about to disappear down the side alley, he added casually, "If you see a cop car, give me a whistle, will you?"

"Er . . . OK." I let my eyes wander up and down the street. I tried to pretend this was normal, but I knew Kenny was frowning.

"Why does he want to know if there are cops around?" he asked.

"Don't know," I said. I had an idea, but I didn't want to say it. I heard dogs barking nearby.

"I don't think this is . . . who is this Nick anyway?"

"He's my friend," I said. "He's the only one who showed up to see me."

"For a good reason. He's using us as lookouts. How long has he been breaking into houses?"

My mouth gaped. "He's not . . . he couldn't be . . ." That's when I heard the sharp tinkle of breaking glass.

"He is," Kenny said. "Let's get out of here."

He shoved me ahead of him, and I started running. Once I started, I felt like I never wanted to stop. My backpack banged against my spine. My breath heaved in my chest, but I kept running . . . past the street where I used to live . . . past my old school . . . past the park . . . past the mall . . . onto the railway platform and into the train that had just stopped at the station. The doors wheezed shut behind me.

I sagged onto the seat, gasping for air. My lungs and throat hurt, but there was another pain deeper inside. I felt nearly as bad as when my bike hit the tree.

I barely heard Kenny puffing beside me. I'd forgotten about him in those crazy minutes of running, but he'd kept up with me.

We got our breath back and sat in silence as the stations slid by, one by one. At the station for the museum we got out and began to walk back to the museum.

"Don't you—"

"Shut up," I snarled.

"Excuse me for living."

We trudged on in silence again, until I couldn't stand it any longer. "Sorry," I muttered.

"Whatever." That was all he said.

Back at the museum, we showed our stamped hands and went inside. We got our notebooks out and began scribbling notes about airplanes and drawing pictures. I hardly knew what I was writing.

Five minutes later, Ben poked his head around the corner. "Where have you guys been? Ms. Crawson's on the warpath."

"Right here," said Kenny.

Ben made a face. "Yeah, sure. You think she's going to believe that? She's been looking all over."

Chapter 6

Saved!

Just then Ms. Crawson appeared, looming up from behind an old, black Model-T car like the ghost of Henry Ford. "Where have you two been?"

"Right here, Ms. Crawson," Kenny said. "We like this part the best. We've done our notes, see?" He held out his notebook. He'd written even faster than I had.

"Now why don't I believe you?" She glared at us suspiciously.

"They were sitting over there behind that airplane, Ms. Crawson. I almost didn't find them." I couldn't believe it. Ben was actually sticking up for us—for me!

"Hmmm. All right, you'd better get down to the cafeteria for lunch," she said.

"Yes, Ms. Crawson," we said in chorus. As we walked down the stairs, I nudged Ben. "Why did you do that?"

"She would've thrown you both off the baseball team. This is the best team we've ever had, so I thought I'd better save you." He grinned, and suddenly I liked him a lot more.

On the bus on the way home, I sat quietly looking out the window as I left the city behind. I was still hurt about my friends, but it was starting to sink in how close I'd come to another disaster.

"What's the matter?" Kenny asked.

"Mom always said I was nothing but trouble. I guess she's right."

"Nah, she's wrong this time." Kenny laughed and punched my arm. "This time you stayed out of trouble, really *big* trouble."

"There's only one problem," I said. "I can't tell her."

And I punched him back, the way friends do.

About the Author

Sherryl Clark

Sherryl Clark has been writing stories, poems, and plays for nearly twenty years. Her first children's book was called *The Too-Tight Tutu*. She teaches writing and editing classes, and also helps people to publish their own books.

Sherryl lives with her husband and her daughter, two cats, and six chickens.

About the Illustrator

Kristin Headlam 

Kristin Headlam is a painter and printmaker, who lives with her dog, Dora Pamphlet. She has regular exhibitions of her work.

To supplement the income of a starving artist, Kristin teaches painting and illustrates books.

Kristin will try anything that comes along, as long as she gets to keep painting.